*Encouragement for the Stay At-home Mom*

*By TeQuila Connors*

*LETTERS TO S.A.M.*

© 2020 by TeQuila Connors



Unless otherwise noted, all scripture quotations are taken from The Holy Bible, New International Version.

ISBN 979-8-81179-756-1
Nonfiction/Family & Relationships/General
Nonfiction/Religion/Inspirational

Authorprenewher Ink @ www.authorprenewher.com
Printed in USA

# ~Dedication~

*This book is dedicated to my beautiful daughter,
Zoi Nyima.*

"It's not the load that breaks you down, it's the way you carry it."

# ~Acknowledgments~

*My Lord and Savior is first and foremost in my heart and mind. If it weren't for Him…, where would I be? I don't have to find out because He is always with me.*

*My Husband, Terry is absolutely amazing. You take care of me as I take care of our little one. You work so hard for our family. I love and appreciate you more than I can say. If no one in the world has my back, I know you do.*

*Zoi's village! You all love on our family and you all come through in so many ways. We appreciate all the prayers, encouragement, resources, and advice (when solicited). We are grateful to have you all helping bring Zoi up in the way that she should go.*

Statements below reflect the feedback of S.A.M.s, Momprenuers and other powerful women that have previewed **Letters to S.A.M.**

*"It is so encouraging, and it held my attention. I have a lot on my plate right now and am seeking for answers. Your book contains content that I need in the instance of birthing anything new. In the end, it pushes me to choose to trust God more and seek His face."*

*- Regina Rather BA, MHSC*

*"This was an amazing read! Whenever I feel alone and misunderstood this will be my go-to! And the prayers came right on time in my spiritual journey! Thank you so much for sharing!"*

*-Divine Destiny 174054*

*Independent*

*Paparazzi Consultant*

"I read your book and I loved it. The way you described everything from before you found out up until after the baby was born was done very well. I felt like I was there with you along the way. This book is a great tool for those wanting to stay home with their children or even those that already stay home with them. I look forward to reading more of your material."

-Kishka M. Gooden
Kishmon Services, LLC


"This book is a true reflection of everything I felt/feel as a stay at- home mother. It took me a whole year just to go back to work and even then, I had so much anxiety about leaving my child with my mom."

-Jarnay Carver
Owner of Maganda Magazine, LLC

*"Thank you for the opportunity to read your new book. It was very interesting to see many of my thoughts and feelings that I have for my children written down on paper."*

*-Aleemah Spence*
*E4 Bookkeeping, LLC*

*"First of all, thank you for writing this. I have had some tough jobs and gone through some hard times, but nothing prepared me for being a Stay At-home Mom. I enjoyed the words of encouragement and the corresponding verses. I found myself making notes for the verses I wanted to meditate on and study. I also liked that the personal stories made me feel like I related to you, but I really appreciated that they were short sections because as you know, it's not common for us to have a lot of time to read. I can picture having 30 minutes out of my day to read and meditate with this book. I would picture notes in the margins and corners turned down so I can*

*reference back to it when I felt like I was falling apart. I already have a good friend that I want to give a copy of this to lol."*

*-Candi Sebera*
*S.A.M. of 2 boys*

Letters
To
S.A.M.

# ~Table of Contents~

Letters
To
S.A.M.

# ~Introduction~

It was a Wednesday evening, and I was on my way home from work. I was talking to my husband on the phone as I normally did. He mentioned that it had been two weeks since my visit to the doctor (she then suggested that we try to conceive because she saw a follicle during my ultrasound). So, he suggested I stop by the drugstore to get a pregnancy test (I got two of them). When I got home, I was anxious and excited. I think we both were because as soon as I walked through the door, he was smiling at me from ear to ear..." You ready?" He asked. I went into the bathroom, followed the instructions and after a few minutes; the stick said PREGNANT! We had been trying for one year and a half; finally, we were pregnant! Many emotions filled us both but the main emotion that we felt was...grateful!

Our plan was always that once we started a family, I would stay home with the children and nurture them to greatness. What I was not prepared for were the feelings and thoughts that came along with taking care of home and child. My emotions were on a constant roller coaster. My thoughts were like a tennis match, I go from positive thought to negative thought; from one side to the other constantly. Some days were more overwhelming than others. I was fulfilled one minute (especially as my baby girl achieved one milestone after another) and then empty the next minute (when the house was quiet, and I was alone with my thoughts). There had been times that I feel the Lord kiss me or hug me. There were times when I received confirmation that He is keeping me and my family; confirmation that I am doing exactly what He planned for my life. These are the moments I felt compelled to share with you, Stay At-home Mom and to reassure you that you are not alone. **In Letters to S.A.M.**, I am sharing moments I needed prayer and encouragement and some of the scriptures that got me through. I am also sharing some of the prayers I spoke over my life. The same confirmations He gave me, belong to you as well.

# I Needed Prayer & Encouragement

I had just left my normal doctor appointment. It went pretty well. They showed me on the monitor that I was having massive contractions, but I wasn't reacting to them as they thought I would (I have a high tolerance for pain). They were saying that I was experiencing pre-labor, but the baby was still not ready to come. I didn't have a problem with that; she wasn't due for another month. I headed right home because my best friend had come up for the weekend for us to have some girl time. My husband was on his way to Dover for weekend duty with the military. She and I decided to go to the pool at my house. It took me forever to decide what bathing suit to wear. I wanted to still look cute with my baby bump, but my options were few. I finally found the right combination of bikini bottom and tank top. As I started to go downstairs, I remembered that I had some cute sunglasses in the car that would set my outfit off! I headed out of the house, to my car and BAM! The pain hit me like lightning! I definitely felt that! I slowly made my way back into the house and told my best friend we may have to reschedule the pool because I was having more pain than usual.

My best friend immediately went into nurse mode, asking questions and calling out commands as I waddled to the downstairs bathroom. She also called my doula to come over and assist her. I was in the bathroom texting my husband. He immediately turned back and started his drive back home. He was about 3 hours away but given the traffic it took him much longer. I was praying, "please don't come while your daddy is away." The pain was off the charts, but I tried to focus on the breathing techniques I had learned over the past couple of months and listened to my best friend and my doula (who by the way got to my house in the speed of light). We stayed at my house for a couple of hours to see if my husband would get there but finally decided to go to the hospital.

I walked around a bit, concentrated on my breathing. The contractions were playing no games. After 3 hours of pre-labor, my water still had not broken so the doctor had to manually break my water. One more hour and it was time to push. My husband had arrived just in time to relieve my best friend. I was squeezing the life out of her hand. After one hour of pushing, our beautiful and healthy 5 pounds 17-ounce baby girl was finally here!!

*"Grow through what you go through."*

His Joy Is Our
Strength

My Child,

The pain of birth is only temporary. Whether it is the birth of a child or the birth of an idea. Once labor is over and the child (finished work) is delivered, you will forget what it took to get to delivery. You will forget the pain you suffered including the feelings of doubt, worry, and frustration. You will only see the results of your labor, a labor of love. So, when the time comes PUSH (Pray Until Somethings Happen) through the pain. I will be right there with you, and we will rejoice together once you have birthed this child (idea).

Your Strength

*John 16:21 (NIV)*
*"A woman giving birth to a child has pain
because her time has come; but when her baby
is born, she forgets the anguish because of
her joy that a child is born into the world."*

My Child,

Rejoice whenever you hear my voice! Receive my words in your heart. Do not let them go in one ear and out of the other. My words are seeds of encouragement and inspiration. Allow the seeds to take root in your heart because that's where they belong. In your heart is where take root and grow. Whenever you face uncertainty or fear; my words will be the fruit inside you nurturing your joy and peace.

Your Strength

*Matthew 13:20 (NIV)*
*"The seed falling on rocky ground refers to someone who hears the word and at once receives it with joy."*

My Child,

I know *trust* can be a scary word sometimes, especially when facing a situation of uncertainty. When I say trust Me, I am saying to allow me to take that situation off your hands. It is just like when you are carrying a load of laundry with your newborn baby on your back. If you allow someone else to carry the laundry for you, your load will become much lighter, and you will be free to move on to the next task; even to play with your little one that is thirsting for your attention. It is ok to let go. It is ok to trust Me…

Your Strength

**Romans 15:13 (NIV)**
**"May the God of hope fill you with
all joy and peace as you trust in him, so that
you may overflow with hope by the power of
the Holy Spirit."**

My Child,

My arms are wide open for you to come and tell me all about it. Use my chest for your head to rest on. Use my shoulder to lean on. Use my sleeve to wipe your tears. I will listen. I will keep your secrets. I will quietly caress your back while you let it all out. Just let it out so that I can replace it with joy.

*Isaiah 51:3 (NIV)*
*"The Lord will surely comfort Zion and will look with compassion on all her ruins; he will make her deserts like Eden, her wastelands like the garden of the Lord. Joy and gladness will be found in her, thanksgiving and the sound of singing."*

My Child,

Others are treating you unfairly. You are persecuted for doing what is right. Allow my joy to guard your heart and mind. You cannot seem to get a break. Your money is short, and worries are long. You are not thinking clearly. Whatever it is, I can take it. I will take it all away and give you joy that will strengthen you to go further.

**1 Thessalonians 1:6 (NIV)**
*"You became imitators of us and of the Lord, for you welcomed the message in the midst of severe suffering with the joy given by the Holy Spirit."*

My Child,

What's that you say? Did you say something? Did you ask a question? I thought I heard you say something. Please don't suffer in silence. Don't go through everyday trials on your own. I am always here listening. I am always willing to give you whatever you ask of Me so that your joy will remain intact. Don't let the cares of this world silence you…Speak up.

Your Strength

*John 16:24 (NIV)*
*"Until now you have not asked for anything
in my name. Ask and you will receive, and
your joy will be complete."*

My Child,

I love it when you sing to me while doing your work around the house. Your voice is a joyful sound to my ears. The praises you sing cause me to wave my hands, keeping all harm from coming your way. The praises you sing cause me to clap my hands, drowning out the noise of this world that tries to overcome you. The praises you sing cause me to sing with you, calling your blessings to rain upon you.

Your Strength

*Psalm 28:7 (NIV)*
*"The Lord is my strength and my shield; my heart trusts in him, and he helps me. My heart leaps for joy, and with my song I praise him."*

My Child,

Today is no different from yesterday. It is a day I have made just for you. A day of goodness and mercy even amid bad news. A day of peace within even when there is sadness all around. A day of joy that is going to keep you strong all day long even though your loved one is no longer with you. So, get up, swing your legs over the bed. Allow your feet to hit the ground. Now stand up. I am your strength to get through this day. Lean on me. I have your loved one. I have you.

Your Strength

**Nehemiah 8:10 (NIV)**
**"This day is holy to our Lord. Do not grieve,**
**for the joy of the Lord is your strength."**

## I Needed Prayer & Encouragement

One of my major obstacles is lack of trust. I believe part of my reason for becoming a Stay At-home Mom is due to my lack of trust in others. I couldn't imagine leaving my child at a daycare facility or with anyone. Let me tell you how bad it was; I wouldn't leave my daughter with her own father. I had so many thoughts going through my head about what could happen while I was away that I built up a legitimate fear in my mind and heart. My husband and I had planned and paid for a cruise for our anniversary. At the time of the cruise, Zoi would have only been 3 months old. This cruise was planned before I knew I was pregnant. I tried to convince myself it would be ok to no avail. Our plan was to leave her with my sister for the week because she was in the position to come to our house and be with her while we were away. I got so worked up that we ended up cancelling the trip and losing half of our money. It was serious!

The first time I left my daughter was when I took some much-needed ME time. My sister drove almost 2 hours to my house to babysit Zoi for an hour. She was six months at the time; maybe seven. I was worried the entire time and she said that Zoi cried for a while, settled into a small wine, and eventually went to sleep. We survived…lol. We tried again the following month for 3 hours. I had attended a very important work event. I was so torn but had to attend. My sister understood my plight, so she kept me apprised by sending pics and texts. The interesting thing was that I was literally eleven minutes away from home.

Eventually, I would take some ME time on some days that my husband was off. I would leave Zoi with him while I go to a doctor appointment or get my nails done. Then came the day to leave my daughter overnight. She was going to be home with her father for one night. I had known the day would come for months and used that time to try to build my courage and dispel my fears. Zoi was a little over 1 year old. My best friend had planned individual boudoir photoshoots for each of us. It was her way of encouraging us to "celebrate our sexy;" a much-needed adventure for sure. The catch was that we had to stay in DC the night before the shoot in order to get there in time the next morning. When she came to pick me up for our trip, I was a mess; but I kissed my little one a whole bunch of times and left the house. I got in the car and cried. I cried from my house to the highway. Stopped crying for a bit until I got alone with my thoughts and cried some more. I had so many mixed emotions. I felt guilty for leaving her, for the reason I left her. I felt nervous my husband wouldn't know what to do when she cried. I was worried she would get hurt. I was still nursing so; I was worried whether what I left for them was going to be enough. The list goes on…

I don't think my husband understood how hard it was for me because he wasn't as responsive as my sister had been. So, it made it even more difficult to be away. I didn't sleep well that night but pushed through my photoshoot. It did take my mind off things for a bit. I had a lot of fun (I recommend it to any of you moms that struggle with the insecurities that come along with our after-pregnancy bodies). I was so appreciative to my Bestie, but I couldn't wait to get back home to my family. I cried when I got back home but again…We survived!

# Please use this space for any thoughts or prayers that come to mind...

# I Needed Prayer & Encouragement

Being a new mom brought joy and excitement as well as fear and anxiety. I didn't know what to do at times and was grateful for those that helped in their own way. The worry and fear came almost immediately when we found out that I was pregnant. I wondered if I would be a good parent. I wondered if I had it in me to do whatever was needed to take care of my child even while she was still in my womb. I had moments of doubt more times than I could count and still do. I pray hardest at night before I go to sleep thanking God, we made it through one more day and hoping for another day to try again.

I found myself worrying if she is sleeping well. If she is happy. In between doctor visits, I am worried if she is healthy and growing properly. I am constantly worried she will get injured. Which she did by the way when she was just 13 months. I was trying on clothes in front of a floor mirror, and she was crawling around on the floor. It slipped my mind that the mirror was broken on the bottom, and she reached up and grabbed it. Sliced her little hand. She was crying and bleeding. I thought I was going to die! I felt so guilty and worried about her. We rushed her to the children's hospital. She had to get stitches…stitches in her little hand! While they were patching her up, I was a ball of nerves. I literally trembled the entire time. The nurse suggested I be given a seductive. Lord! Needless to say, this situation amplified my fear of her getting hurt. The good thing that came out of it was she started walking within a week after the injury because she had a hard time crawling using one hand.

He Is Our
Peace

My Child,

Here. Let peace be yours for the keeping. Let it reside within your heart. I have given you peace as a gift, but it is your choice to accept this present. Today things are going to happen that are out of your control. You cannot change this, so I want you to always be at peace. No matter what things look like around you. No matter how overwhelming things may seem. Let my peace reside in your heart and let that peace flow through you. Let my peace today remain your present.

Your Peace

*John 16:33 (NIV)*
*"I have told you these things, so that in me*
*you may have peace. In this world you will*
*have trouble. But take heart! I have overcome*
*the world."*

My Child,

My peace is not just for everyone else. It is also your destiny. It is your right to be at peace, always. So, whatever you need to do to feel the peace that I have given to you…do it. Spend some time with Me. Go; take a spa day, unwind with your favorite book, take a trip, and enjoy some "Me time" or "Mommy time." Allow yourself to be rejuvenated by a scoop of your favorite ice cream. It will be difficult for you to take care of your family if you don't take care of You. Once you have had your time of refreshing, you can get back to be the awesome S.A.M. that you are.

Your Peace

**I sometimes enjoy a McDonalds ice cream cone as my "Mommy time" getaway. It's the little things…*

*Colossians 3:15 (NIV)*
*"Let the peace of Christ rule in your hearts,*
*since as members of one body you were called*
*to peace. And be thankful."*

My Child,

Pray and don't worry. Bills will come every month. Children cry when they don't know the words to say how they feel. Not everyone is going to understand what you are going through. You may not always know what your next step will be but don't worry. You may be in a situation and not know who to call; call on Me. The kind of peace I give you will calm your thoughts and clear your mind. Your family and friends may even wonder in amazement how you get it all done. How you can smile and encourage others when things appear rough for you. Tell them to sing with you; "Don't worry about a thing…every little thing is gonna be alright."

Your Peace

*Philippians 4:6-7 (NIV)*
*"Do not be anxious about anything, but in every situation, by prayer and petition, with thanksgiving, present your requests to God. And the peace of God, which transcends all understanding, will guard your hearts and your minds in Christ Jesus."*

My Child,

You are Mine. Just as you will do anything for your family; I will do anything for you. Be at peace because even when you don't feel strong, I will give you strength. Others may even wonder how you are able to do all that you do when your plate seems so full. You are a mom, wife, entrepreneur, the list goes on. I have given you what you need to get it all done. I have given you Strength and Peace. You...Got...This because I've...Got...You.

Your Peace

**Psalm 29:11 (NIV)**
**"The Lord gives strength to his people;**
**the Lord blesses his people with peace."**

My Child,

Look at you! You are amazing! You are organized, focused, and at peace. Keep up that go-getter spirit! This peace will sustain you and keep you healthy. You will wake everyday refreshed and rejuvenated with lots to do but not a care in the world. You go, Girl!

Your Peace

**Proverbs 14:30 (NIV)**
*"A heart at peace gives life to the body, but
envy rots the bones."*

My Child,

There is absolutely nothing wrong with discipline. Correction builds character in your child. Put in the work now of discipline and correction so that you will have less work later when they are older. Remain fair, firm and just. Let my actions be your example and teach your little one all that you learn from Me. A child that has learned right from wrong will grow up to make you proud; just as I am proud of you, everyday!

Your Peace

*Proverbs 29:17 (NIV)*
*"Discipline your children, and they will give you peace; they will bring you the delights you desire."*

My Child,

Peace, I write to you because I have overcome this world and all that it may throw your way. Just let me know what you want me to do, and I will do it. I will watch you while you sleep so peacefully each night. When you awake in the morning, I will hand you all the goodness and mercy you need throughout your day, so you lack nothing.

*Romans 15:33 (NIV)*
*"The God of peace be with you all. Amen."*

"When we put our problems in God's hands,
he puts His peace in our hearts."

## Please use this space for any thoughts or prayers that come to mind...

## I Needed Prayer & Encouragement

I had an agreement with my supervisor that allowed me to be on maternity leave until my daughter was 6 months. Leave did not start after I had my daughter. I continued to work from the hospital and when we got home. After a few months of working from home and learning to be a mom, my supervisor asked me to come back to work. She and my manager said people were beginning to talk and wondering if I was ever coming back to work. I was just starting to get into a rhythm of being a mom and working from home. I expressed that this was not the agreement (which was in writing) and that I had been working the entire time (in the hospital and at home). I had not actually had maternity leave. It was then suggested that I bring my daughter to work with me and turn my office into an office/nursery until I was ready to send her to daycare. I was extremely annoyed but also grateful. I expressed that this setup was almost unheard of and an ideal situation for anyone in my position, but it felt a bit unorthodox. Nevertheless, I agreed. This went on for another 6 months. I was stressed because I was practically working two full-time jobs at the same time. Not to mention, I was supposed to stop working all together once she was born. Well, the waters were troubled again. My supervisor passed away and the stuff hit the fan. There were others that I worked with indirectly that began to tear down everything positive she had put into place during her tenure. The employee morale took a turn for bad among other things. While others and I were still grieving her loss, I was told to find childcare because people were uncomfortable coming to my office with a child there and others were beginning to talk about how unfair it was that I had my child with me at work. I was angry, sad, and unsure. Although she was a little over 1 year old, I was not ready to put my daughter in childcare. I submitted my letter of resignation. I needed to return to the original plan of being a Stay At-home Mom.

*"Being a mother is learning about strengths you didn't know you had and dealing with fears you never knew existed."*
*- Linda Wooten*

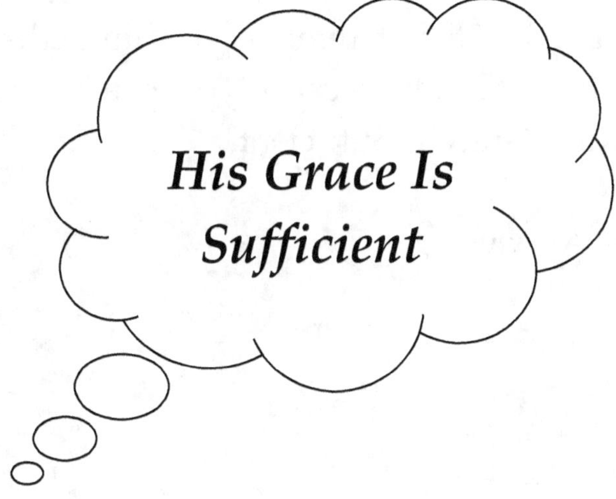
His Grace Is
Sufficient

My Child,

Things tend to pile up and get out of your control. When things are out of your control, you feel helpless and weak. It isn't as bad as it seems. My grace is with you and will strengthen you to continue. You will get tired, you will feel overwhelmed, but you will get through. I will not remove you immediately from the situation because you need to learn this…My Grace Is Sufficient.

Yours Always

*2 Corinthians 12:9 (NIV)*
*"But he said to me, "My grace is sufficient for you, for my power is made perfect in weakness." Therefore, I will boast all the more gladly about my weaknesses, so that Christ's power may rest on me."*

My Child,

Yes, it does seem like your family has been singled out. Yes, it does seem like you have a bull's-eye on your back. No, I will not leave you alone in your time of need. No, I will not leave you to go through without a comforter. Whatever happens to you and your family are the same things that happen to My other children. Tests and trials come to give you a glimpse of my plans. I have my intended outcome for you, written in a book. As the pages turn, life will throw things your way. No matter what page you are on…know that the situation will end in your favor. You will triumph!

Yours Always

*Jeremiah 29:11(MSG)*
*"I know what I'm doing. I have it all planned out – plans to take care of you, not abandon you, plans to give you the future you hope for."*

My Child,

As a Stay At-home Mom you have a lot to contend. You have a lot of plans to make. You wear many hats; a mom, nurse, teacher, and much more. You must be organized, composed, goal oriented, and steadfast. I am aware of your plans, and I want you to know that I am in your corner. I will ensure your plans go smoothly.

Yours Always

*Proverbs 16:1 (NIV)*
*"To humans belong the plans of the heart, but from the Lord comes the proper answer of the tongue."*

My Child,

Daily, you strive for excellence. Daily, you do what it takes to care for your family. When you persuade a bill collector to settle for a lower amount; good for you. When you clip coupons to save on the grocery bill; good for you. When you stay up all night with a sick baby and still ensure breakfast is ready in the morning; good for you. You constantly strive for excellence and do what it takes to care for your family. So...what do _You_ want? Just ask and it is yours. Allow me to take care of you now. I always will.

Yours Always

**Psalm 20:5 (NIV)**
*"May we shout for joy over your victory and lift up our banners in the name of our God. May the Lord grant all your requests."*

My Child,

This is a *big deal*. Being a Stay At-home Mom is a *big deal*. I chose you because you are a *big deal*. Children are my most precious gifts. Raising a child does not come with a manual or a template. You have no way of gauging whether you are doing it right or not, but you *are* doing it. You are doing great just like I knew you would. I chose you for this. I've equipped you for this. You are something special…You got this!

Yours Always

*1 Thessalonians 1:4-5 (MSG)*
*"...It is clear to us, friends, that God not only loves you very much but also has put his hand on you for something special."*

My Child,

Before you say a word, let me get that for you. Before you finish that sentence, let me take care of it. I see you when you get tired, when you get weary, when things get so tough; you want to scream. Let me take care of it for you.

Yours Always

*Isaiah 65:24 (NIV)*
*"Before they call, I will answer; while they are still speaking, I will hear."*

My Child,

You choosing to be a Stay At-home Mom compels me to make sure you live your days in prosperity and pleasure. You have taken on a monumental task; please trust that I will help you. You are such a blessing to your family. Trust that whatever I ask you to do, that it will lead to your success. Some things that I bring before you can be hard tasks, they may even seem impossible, but trust Me. Trust Me without fear and things will go smoother than you anticipate.

Yours Always

Proverbs 3:5-6 (NIV)
"Trust in the Lord with all your heart and
lean not on your own understanding; in all
your ways submit to him, and he will make
your paths straight."

My Child,

You don't know how good you have it, do you? You have me wrapped around your finger. Just like your child has you wrapped around his/her little finger. When that little one looks up at you with expectation and love; you just melt. You will give him/her anything he/she asks within reason. It is my will that you are blessed and prosperous. Have confidence that anything you ask of me will be yours.

Yours Always

*1 John 5:14 (NIV)*
*"This is the confidence we have in approaching God: that if we ask anything according to his will, he hears us."*

My Child,

I saw it when your only source of transportation was towed in the middle of the night, and you had to take the bus to your child's doctor appointment. I saw when your best friend stabbed you in the back over money. I saw when your baby father left you for someone else. I saw when the doctor diagnosed you with breast cancer and said that he did not know what to do for you. I know you would rather none of these things happen to you. All that was taken will be returned to you in double. All that was broken will be replaced with a higher quality model. All that the doctor says is wrong with you, I will make it right. Do not fear. Do not worry. We are in this together.

Yours Always

**Psalm 112:7 (NIV)**
**"They will have no fear of bad news; their hearts are steadfast, trusting in the Lord."**

My Child,

It is my wish always for you to be healthy. Not only physical health but mental and spiritual health as well. I will provide for you a balanced diet of spiritual food and physical food, daily. I cherish you, My Love. I will always root for your prosperity and pleasure until you depart this natural realm and return home to me.

Yours Always

*3 John 1:2 (NKJV)*
*"Beloved, I pray that you may prosper in all things and be in health, just as your soul prospers."*

# Please use this space for any thoughts or prayers that come to mind...

# The Prayer Closet

A Stay At-home Mom should be prayed up. Never leave a prayer unspoken. Never leave an area of your life uncovered by prayer. We certainly do not have a shortage of things to pray about. The pages to follow are just a few of the prayers that I have written down and have prayed many times over. We may not always have the opportunity to go into our prayer closet, but we can pray whenever we feel the need, as often as we need, and for whatever we need. Just remember not to close your eyes while you are driving…lol

## Morning prayer

Thank you, Lord, for this day
Forgive me of my sins I pray
Things are gonna go my way
Thank you for this day

In Your Name, Amen

**I say this one with my daughter every morning. She is now 2 years old and almost has it memorized*

**Prayer to remember You**

Heavenly Father,

I can get so consumed daily that I forget what you are to me. I forget that you are my source, my sustainer, and my strength. You are always thinking of me. When I sleep you stay awake taking care of everything, I have worried about throughout the day. Please help me to remember that you are my everything.

In Your Name, Amen

## Prayer over spouse/baby father

Thank you, Heavenly Father, for your grace. Thank you, Lord God that it is by your grace we are saved. I ask you now Father to watch over my husband (baby father) as the day goes on. Keep your hedge of protection around him. Bring him into the company of those that can use their power, abilities, gifts, and influence to help him along the path you have laid before him. Give him a clear vision for this family and I thank you that along with the vision, you provide provisions. Bless the works of his hands…always.

In Your Name, Amen

**Prayer over children**

Heavenly Father,

I thank you for believing in me. I thank you for blessing me to be a steward over my child(children). Grant me the wisdom to make the right decisions as it pertains to my child(children). I pray that they are always happy, healthy, and humble. Help me to show them your love in my words and actions. I pray for their understanding that discipline and correction are not bad but necessary. I pray for their minds to be nourished as well as their bodies. Help me to not fear for them while they are away from me because you are with them.

In Your Name, Amen

## Blessing over home

Heavenly Father,

I invite you into this home. You are our provider and our source. You have blessed us with this home to protect this family from the elements. The blood of Jesus is on every door post keeping any spirits that are not of You from entering. I pray for every wall, every doorknob, the floor, and the ceiling to be upheld by your grace. The foundation of this home is built upon your rock. Let the memories of this home be more joyous than not. Bless those that bless our household. Please continue to rain favor over this house.

In Your Name, Amen

## Prayer for finances

Heavenly Father,

There is nothing that I can go through that is new to You. There is a season for everything including a season to sow and a season to reap. I thank You, Father that I have seed in the ground that has and continues to produce a harvest for my family. I thank you that you are concerned about all that concerns me. I understand that bills are the cost of our needs, living in this world. I am so grateful that you provide for our every need according to your riches in glory through Christ Jesus. You will not see us forsaken and I thank you, Father.

In Your Name, Amen

## Prayer for health

Heavenly Father,

Thank you for knowing all about me, even the number of hairs on my head. You are my healer whenever dis-ease comes my way. I know that it is your wish that I am always healthy mentally, physically as well as spiritually. Thank you for giving me the wisdom to care for my family. It is by Jesus' stripes that we are all healed and healthy. For that alone…I thank You!

In Your Name, Amen

## Prayer for reassurance

Heavenly Father,

I have so much to do but also feel sometimes that I am doing nothing. I often feel unhappy because I don't think I am helping my family. I don't think I am helping anyone. I go to sleep at night just to wake up to the same routine every day. I realize that happiness is external, and I shouldn't expect to be happy all the time. Help me to stay joyful, Father. Help me to know that what I do matters. Your joy is my strength and with every new day there is new mercy and grace to reassure me.

In Your Name, Amen

**Bedtime prayer**

Heavenly Father,

I thank you for this day that you have made. This was a day I had never seen before, but it was full of blessings because I was still in it. Calm my thoughts and clear my mind. Help me rest peacefully at bedtime. Forgive me of any sins I may have committed knowingly and unknowingly. I pray that you grant me grace to see another day. I love you, Father for you are with me always.

In Your Name, Amen

**Please use this space for any thoughts or prayers that come to mind...**

*"Chaos is not a sign of failure, it's a sign of children."*    *- Paula Rollo*

# ~Scripture References~

## His Joy Is Our Strength

John 16:21, Matthew 13:20, Romans 15:13, Isaiah 51:3, 1 Thessalonians 1:6, John 16:24, Psalm 28:7, Nehemiah 8:10

## He Is Our Peace

John 16:33, Colossians 3:15, Philippians 4:6-7, Psalm 29:11, Proverbs 14:30, Proverbs 29:17, Romans 15:33

## His Grace Is Sufficient

2 Corinthians 12:9, Jeremiah 29:11 MSG, Proverbs 16:1, Psalm 20:5, 1 Thessalonians 1:4-5 MSG, Isaiah 65:24, Proverbs 3:5-6, 1 John 5:14, Psalm 112:7, 3 John 1:2 NKJV

** Unless otherwise noted, all scripture quotations are taken from The Holy Bible, New International Version.*

**P.S...** Thank you, S.A.M. for sharing in these love notes from our Heavenly Father. It is my prayer that you are further encouraged that being a Stay At-home Mom is rewarding and you were hand-picked for the job. It may seem at times that you are not appreciated or valued (even by You). But I believe there is a special place in Gods heart for the mother. Your labors of love are not going unnoticed. Stay encouraged. Stay before Him in prayer. Stay amazing.

# ~About the Author~

TeQuila Connors is a native of Virginia. She is an entrepreneur and published author. TeQuila enjoys reading and has become a creative poet and intuitive writer over the last two decades. She has just in recent years decided to transform her writings into books and to help others do the same with her publishing company, Authorprenewher Ink.

After giving birth to her daughter Zoi, TeQuila attempted to continue working but along with her husband's persuasion and the pull of the Holy Spirit, she walked away from her full-time job and became a Stay At-home Mom/Mompreneur. One day, while going about her busy day (publishing business, being a wife and homemaker, and caring after her wonderful bundle of love) she felt an overwhelming gratefulness and peace.

Regardless of the tasks at hand, she knew that the Holy Spirit was comforting her. She also knew that other Stay At-home Moms needed to feel what she felt in that moment. Receive your comfort from these pages.

Receive reassurance from these pages. Know that He Is Our Peace, His Joy Is Our Strength, and His Grace is Sufficient!

Other Works by TeQuila

*Love Is Air: poetry*
*The Seed: how to grow spiritually to a fruitful tree*
*To You, From Him: love notes from God*

Purchase your autographed copies via
http://authorprenewher.com

Contact:
tkconnors@authorprenewher.com
Instagram @tkconnors
Facebook @authortkconnors

www.ingramcontent.com/pod-product-compliance
Lightning Source LLC
Chambersburg PA
CBHW072105150726
47999CB00005B/1901